Countries of the World

Canada

by Michael Dahl

Ms. Marshall

Content Consultant:
Harriett Goldsborough
Canadian Education Association

Bridgestone Books
an Imprint of Capstone Press

Bridgestone Books are published by Capstone Press
1710 Roe Crest Drive, North Mankato, Minnesota 56003
www.capstonepress.com

102012
006949R

Library of Congress Cataloging-in-Publication Data
Dahl, Michael
    Canada/by Michael Dahl.
    p. cm.--(Countries of the world)
    Includes bibliographical references and index.
    Summary: Discusses the history, landscape, people, animals, and culture of the country
of Canada.
        ISBN-10: 1-56065-565-8 (hardcover)   ISBN-13: 978-1-56065-565-7 (hardcover)
        ISBN-10: 0-7368-8368-1 (softcover)   ISBN-13: 978-0-7368-8368-9 (softcover)
        1. Canada--Juvenile literature. [1. Canada.] I. Title. II. Series: Countries of the world
(Mankato, Minn.)
F1008.2.D35   1998
917.1--dc21

                                                        97-5815
                                                         CIP
                                                         AC

Photo credits
Brian Beck, 12
Capstone Press, 5 (left)
Firth Photobank, cover
Protestant School Board of Greater Montreal, Media Services/Alan Taylor, 10
Root Resources/Alan Nelson, 14
James Rowan, 18
Unicorn Stock/Jim Shippee, 5 (right); Margo Moss, 6; Karen Mullen, 16; A. Ramey, 20
Brian A. Vikander, 8

Table of Contents

Fast Facts

Name: Canada

Capital: Ottawa, in the province of Ontario

Population: More than 28 million

Languages: English, French

Religions: Roman Catholic, Protestant

Size: 3,988,244 square miles (10,369,434 square kilometers) *Canada is the second largest country in the world.*

Crops: Wheat, lumber, canola oil

Maps

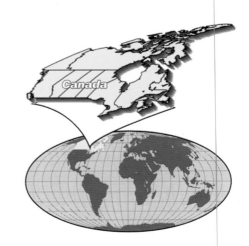

Flag

Canada's flag is mainly red. In the middle of the flag is a white square. A red maple leaf is on this square. The maple tree is the national tree of Canada. Red and white are Canada's national colors. This design became Canada's flag in 1965. Thousands of designs were considered for the flag. The maple leaf was the final choice. People felt the maple leaf stood for all Canadians.

Currency

The unit of currency in Canada is the Canadian dollar. It takes 100 cents to equal one dollar. Canada also has one- and two-dollar coins.

The amount of Canadian money it takes to make a U.S. dollar changes daily.

The Land of Canada

Canada is a large country north of the United States. It is the second largest country in the world. It also has the longest coastline. Coastline is land by a lake or an ocean. Traveling Canada's coastline would be like traveling around Earth six times. English and French are Canada's two languages.

Canada has 10 provinces. A province is an area that makes up a country. It is like a state in the United States. Canada also has three territories. A territory is land under the control of a nation.

The Atlantic, Pacific, and Arctic Oceans touch Canada's borders. The Rocky Mountains cover part of western Canada. Large rivers flow into Hudson Bay in eastern Canada. Canada also has many lakes, streams, and forests. Most large cities are in southern Canada. About 60 percent of Canada's people live in the southern part of the country.

Canada's name comes from the Native American work kanata. Kanata means community.

Canada has many forests, lakes, and mountains.

First Canadians

Inuit (IN-oo-it) people are natives of northern Canada. They were once known as Eskimos. Inuit people were the first people in Canada.

In 1534, French explorer Jacques Cartier (Zhahck Car-tee-ay) sailed up Canada's St. Lawrence River. An explorer is someone who travels to faraway places. An explorer wants to learn about the new places.

Soon more people came into Canada. They discovered rivers and built buildings. Today, many of the places these people settled have grown into major cities.

Canadian wilderness is important, too. Wilderness is land where few or no people live. The wilderness is covered with lakes and forests. People use some of the trees. Workers cut down trees and send them to paper mills. Canada's factories make most of the world's paper. Canadian trees are also used to build houses.

Inuit people are natives of northern Canada.

Going to School

Each Canadian province is in charge of its own schools. This is why many Canadian schools have different rules. Because Canada has two languages, students learn English and French.

Canada's public schools offer free eduction. People must pay to go to private schools. Most Canadian children go to elementary school from age six to 12. They go to middle school from age 12 to 14. Canadian high schools are for students from age 15 to 17 or 18.

Native American groups in Canada are called First Nations. Some First-Nations people live on reserves in northern Canada. A reserve is Canadian land set aside for First-Nations people. They often have their own schools.

Sometimes Canada's northern schools are far away from student's homes. Then students can learn from their teacher by using a computer. Other students write back and forth to teachers.

Canada's public schools offer free education.

Canadian Food

Canadians come from many different cultures. A culture is a way of life for a group of people. A culture includes people's ideas and special practices. Each culture has favorite foods.

Butter tarts are a popular treat in Canada. Tarts are like cookies. They are made with butter, raisins, and brown sugar.

Special pea soup is a favorite food of some French Canadians. Tourtière is a food eaten on Christmas Eve. Tourtière is pork pie.

Fish is a popular food in the Atlantic provinces. It is also a main food of the Inuit people. Today, most Inuit live in northern Canada. They sometimes fish and hunt for food.

Another Canadian treat is maple syrup. It is made from the sap of a maple tree. People turn the sap into sweet maple syrup. Some people use the sap to make maple sugar candy. They make maple syrup pies, too.

People gather sap from maple trees.

Animals in Canada

Canada's large countryside is home to thousands of wild animals. One-fourth of the world's grizzly bears live in Canada. Polar bears live in Canada, too. They hunt in the cold, northern areas of Canada.

Bald eagles fly high above forests. Groups of musk ox and caribou live on far northern land. Moose and deer live in the woods.

Geese fly above lakes. Seals hunt in Canada's icy oceans. Dolphins and humpback whales swim in the water off Canada's shores.

Canada's northern waterways are home to the narwhal. The narwhal is a whale with a long, sharp tooth. The tooth sticks out in front like a horn.

Polar bears hunt in northern Canada.

Canadian Sports

Canada has many wilderness ares. People visit Canada's wilderness to enjoy nature. Many visitors hunt or fish. Some people ski on snowy mountain slopes. Others canoe on rivers. Families camp in Canada's 31 national parks.

Lacrosse is Canada's national sport. It is a game Canadians learned from First-Nations. people. Lacrosse is played on a grassy field. Players use long sticks with nets on the end. They carry and pass the ball with the sticks.

Hockey is one of Canada's most popular sports. Young children play in hockey clubs all across the country. Hockey, swimming, baseball, and skiing are the four most played sports.

Ice-skating is another popular sport in Canada. People ice-skate on frozen lakes and streams. There are also indoor places to ice-skate in most cities and towns.

Many people fish on lakes in Canada's wilderness.

Cities, Roads, and Trains

Most Canadians live in busy, modern cities. Ottawa, Ontario, is the capital of Canada. Most people in Ottawa speak both English and French. Toronto, Ontario, is the largest city in Canada.

Montreal, Quebec, is another major city in Canada. Most people in Montreal speak French. It is the world's second largest French-speaking city. Only Paris, France, is larger.

Roads, trains, and planes are important because Canada is so large. The Trans-Canada Highway stretches from east to west. The highway is 5,000 miles (8,000 kilometers) long.

Canada also has more than 52,000 miles (83,200 kilometers) of railroad track. Workers help keep Canada's trains running smoothly during hard winter.s

Highways, planes, and railways help people in wilderness areas receive supplies. They let people from cities travel and enjoy nature.

Canada's trains help people travel in wilderness areas.

Royal Canadian Mounties

Canada is known for its Royal Canadian Mounted Police. This is Canada's national police force. The force helps make sure people obey the laws of Canada. Police officers are often called Mounties.

Mounties are known by their bright red uniforms. They also wear special wide-brimmed hats. They wear black boots, too.

Long ago, Mounties rode on horseback. They had large ares of wilderness to patrol. Patrol means to travel around an area and protect it. There are more than 20,000 Mounties in Canada today. Most modern Mounties drive squad cars.

Mounties try to keep Canada safe They are the local police for about 200 towns and villages. They are also the local police force in all provinces and territories except Ontario and Quebec. Ontario and Quebec have their own local police forces. But Mounties still make sure people in Ontario and Quebec follow Canada's national laws.

Mounties are known by their bright red uniforms.

Hands On: Make a Totem Pole

Some First-Nations people on Canada's West Coast make totem poles. A totem pole is a specially shaped and painted wooden pole. People usually carve animals and plants on their totem poles. These carvings stand for their family. You can make your own totem pole.

What You Need

Five to 10 empty cans of the same size
Sheets of colored paper
Markers, crayons, or pens
Glue
Scissors

What You Do

1. Cover the cans with the colored paper. Decorate each can. Make faces of yourself or friends. You could also make a can look like a favorite animal.
2. Glue pictures or special objects to your cans.
3. Put glue on the top of each can. Stack the cans on top of each other. The glue will keep them together.

Change or add cans from time to time. Add new cans for special holidays. Trade cans with friends. Make their cans part of your totem pole.

Learn to Speak French

good	bon	(bohn)
good-bye	au revoir	(oh ruh-vwah)
good morning	bonjour	(bohn-joor)
or **good day**		
great	grand	(grahn)
no	non	(nohn)
please	s'il vous plaît	(seel voo play)
sorry	désolé	(day-zoh-lay)
thank you	merci	(mare-see)
yes	oui	(wee)

Words to Know

culture (KUHL-chur)—a way of life for a group of people

Inuit (IN-oo-it)—people from the Arctic north of Canada, Alaska, and Greenland; they were once known as Eskimos.

province (PROV-uhnss)—an area that makes up a country

reserve (ri-ZURV)—Canadian land set aside for First-Nations people

territory (TER-uh-tor-ee)—land under the control of a country

Read More

Barlas, Bob and Norm Tompsett. *Canada*. Milwaukee: Gareth Stevens, 1997.

Hamilton, Janice. *Canada*. Globe-Trotter Club. Minneapolis: Carolrhoda Books, 1999.

Internet Sites

FactHound offers a safe, fun way to find Internet sites related to this book.

Go to *www.facthound.com*

He'll fetch the best sites for you!

Index